The Overhaul

Kathleen Jamie

The Overhaul

POEMS

GRAYWOLF PRESS

First published by Picador, an imprint of Pan Macmillan, a division of
Macmillan Publishers Limited, London.

This publication is made possible, in part, by the voters of Minnesota through
a Minnesota State Arts Board Operating Support grant, thanks to a legislative
appropriation from the arts and cultural heritage fund, and through grants
from the National Endowment for the Arts and the Wells Fargo Foundation
Minnesota. Significant support has also been provided by Target, the McKnight
Foundation, Amazon.com, and other generous contributions from foundations,
corporations, and individuals. To these organizations and individuals we offer
our heartfelt thanks.

Published by Graywolf Press
250 Third Avenue North, Suite 600
Minneapolis, Minnesota 55401

www.graywolfpress.org

Published in the United States of America

ISBN 978-1-55597-702-3

2 4 6 8 9 7 5 3 1
First Graywolf Printing, 2015

Library of Congress Control Number: 2014950980

Cover design: Jeenee Lee Design

Cover art: *Shetland Fourern,* linocut by James Dodds

for P. and D. and F.

Contents

The Overhaul

The Beach

Now this big westerly's
blown itself out,
let's drive to the storm beach.

A few brave souls
will be there already,
eyeing the driftwood,

the heaps of frayed
blue polyprop rope,
cut loose, thrown back at us –

What a species –
still working the same
curved bay, all of us

hoping for the marvellous,
all hankering for a changed life.

The Dash

Every mid-February
those first days arrive
when the sun rises
higher than the Black
Hill at last. Brightness
and a crazy breeze
course from the same airt –
turned clods gleam, the trees'
topmost branches bend
shivering downwind.
They chase, this lithe pair
out of the far south
west, and though scalding
to our wintered eyes
look, we cry, *it's here*

Five Tay Sonnets

1. OSPREYS

You'll be wondering why you bothered: beating
up from Senegal, just to hit a teuchit storm –
late March blizzards and raw winds – before the tilt

across the A9, to arrive, mere
hours apart, at the self-same riverside

Scots pine, and possess again the sticks and fishbones
of last year's nest: still here, pretty much
like the rest of us – gale-battered, winter-worn,
        half toppled away . . .

So redd up your cradle, on the tree-top,
claim your teind from the shining
estates of the firth, or the trout-stocked loch.
What do you care? Either way,
there'll be a few glad whispers round town today:
that's them, baith o' them, they're in.

2. Springs

Full March moon and gale-force easters, the pair of them
sucking and shoving the river
back into its closet in the hills, or trying to. Naturally

the dykes failed, the town's last fishing boat
raved at the pier-head, then went down; diesel-
corrupted water cascaded into front-yards, coal-holes, garages,

and *there's naethin ye can dae*,
said the old boys, the sages, which may be true; but river –
what have you left us? Evidence of an inner life, secrets
of your estuarine soul hawked halfway

up Shore Street, up East and Mid Shore, and arrayed
in swags all through the swing-park: plastic trash and broken reeds,
driftwood, bust TVs . . .
                                  and a salmon,
dead, flung beneath the see-saw, the crows are onto at once.

3. MAY

Again the wild blossom
powering down at dusk, the gean trees
a lather at the hillfoot
                    and a blackbird, telling us
what he thinks to it, telling us
                    what he thinks . . .
How can we bear it? A fire-streaked sky, a firth
decked in gold, the grey clouds passing
like peasant-folk
                    lured away by a prophecy.
                                        What can we say
the blackbird's failed
to iterate already? Night calls:
the windows of next-door's glass house
crimson, then go mute

4. EXCAVATION & RECOVERY

Then specialists arrived, in hi-viz jackets and hardhats
who floundered out every low tide
to the log-boat, lodged
in the mud since the Bronze Age. Eventually

it was floated to the slipway, swung high
in front of our eyes: black, dripping, aboriginal
– an axe-hewn hollowed-out oak
            sent to the city on a truck.

What were you to them, river, who hollered
'Shipping water!' or 'Ca' canny lads!' in some now
long-forgotten tongue?

an estuary with a discharge of 160 cubic metres of water per second
as per the experts' report?
or Tay/Toi/Taum   – a goddess;
                        the Flowing(?), the Silent One(?).

5. 'Doing Away'

Nowhere to go, nowhere I'd rather be
than here, fulfilling my daily rituals.
                         Why would one want
to absent oneself, when one's commute

is a lonely hillside by-way, high
above the river? Specially when the tide's
way out, leaving the firth
like a lovers' bed with the sheets stripped back

baring its sandbanks, its streamy rivulets,
– the whole thing shining
like an Elfland, and all a mere two fields'
stumbling walk away . . .

Someday I'll pull into a passing-place
a mile from home, and leave the car,

           when they find it
                engine thrumming quietly

Fragment 1

Roe deer,
   breaking from a thicket

bounding over briars
   between darkening trees

you don't even glance
   at the cause of your doubt

so how can you tell
   what form I take?

What form I take
   I scarcely know myself

adrift in a wood
   in wintertime at dusk

always a deer
   breaking from a thicket

for a while now
   this is how it's been

Fragment 2

Imagine we could begin
all over again; begin

afresh, like this February
dawn light, coaxing

from the Scots pines
their red ochre, burnt-earth glow.

All over again. South
– facing mountainsides, balcony

above balcony of pines – imagine
we could mend

whatever we heard fracture:
splintering of wood, a bird's

cry over still water, a sound
only reaching us now

The Longhouse

Who lives here? Don't
you remember that hill? How it
shut out any winter sun –
or those ash trees
sheltering the gable end?

Hefted to its own land
like its few yowes –

Today the wind's swung north –
in overcoats and headscarves
two women are crossing the yard

As if yoked together,
they stall, and turn to face us –

and though you look
from one to the other,
one to the other,
you just can't tell

which is daughter, which mother . . .

This is what happens.
This is why we loosed our grip and fled

like the wind-driven smoke
from the single lum
in the crooked roof that covers
both women and beasts, a roof
low and broken like a cry

The Study

Moon,

      what do you mean,
entering my study
like a curiosity shop,
stroking in mild concern

the telescope mounted
on its tripod, the books,
the attic stair? You
who rise by night, who draw

the inescapable world
closer, a touch,
to your gaze – why
query me? What's mine

is yours; but you've no more
need of those implements
than a deer has,
browsing in a glade.

Moon, your work-
worn face bright
outside unnerves me.
Please, be on your way.

Hawk and Shadow

I watched a hawk
glide low across the hill,
her own dark shape
in her talons like a kill.

She tilted her wings,
fell into the air –
the shadow coursed on
without her, like a hare.

Being out of sorts
with my so-called soul,
part unhooked hawk,
part shadow on parole,

I played fast and loose:
keeping one in sight
while forsaking the other.
The hawk gained height:

her mate on the ground
began to fade,
till hill and sky were empty,
and I was afraid.

The Stags

This is the multitude, the beasts
you wanted to show me, drawing me
upstream, all morning up through wind-
scoured heather to the hillcrest.
Below us, in the next glen, is the grave
calm brotherhood, descended
out of winter, out of hunger, kneeling
like the signatories of a covenant;
their weighty, antique-polished antlers
rising above the vegetation
like masts in a harbour, or city spires.
We lie close together, and though the wind
whips away our man-and-woman smell, every
stag-face seems to look toward us, toward,
but not to us: we're held, and hold them,
in civil regard. I suspect you'd
hoped to impress me, to lift to my sight
our shared country, lead me deeper
into what you know, but loath
to cause fear you're already moving
quietly away, sure I'll go with you,
as I would now, almost anywhere.

Highland Sketch

Another landscape,

another swept glen,
more roadside wildflowers
breezing through their season
and round the next bend
 − lo! another sea-loch
shot with nets of aquamarine . . .
        We're old enough, dear friend,
not to need to explain, not,
at least, to each other:
− sufficient years between us
to recognize, raked
down the threadbare hillsides
long-forsaken lazy-beds
where a crop was raised.
        − We don't make love,
we read a while,
leaf through a book
of 19th century photographs:
hands like stones,
shy, squinting faces
admonish us.
We really ought to rouse ourselves
to greet some weather −
now westlin' winds, now shrouded bens
now a late sklent of sunlight to the heart.

A Raised Beach

– of course, that's what –
a plain of stones, perfectly
smooth and still
showing the same slight
ridges and troughs
as thousands of years ago
when the sea left.
– It *is* a sea – even grey
stones one can
walk across: not a
solitary flower, nor a single
blade of grass –
   I know this place
– all with one face
accepting of the sun
the other . . . Moon,
why have you turned to me
your dark side, why am I
examining these stones?
Our friendship lapsed.
– And sea, dear mother,
retreating with long stealth
though I lie awake –
Ah, you're a grown-up now
I've sung to you
quite long enough.

Swifts

When we first emerged, we assumed
what we'd entered
was the world,
and we its only creatures.

Soon, we could fly; soon
we'd mastered its grey gloom,
could steal a single
waterdrop

even as it fell.
Now you who hesitate,
fearful of the tomb-smell,

fearful of shades,
look up – higher!
How deft we are,

how communicative, our
scorch-brown wings almost
translucent against the blue.

Deserts, moonlit oceans, heat
climbing from a thousand coastal cities
are as nothing now,

say our terse screams.
The cave-dark we were born in
calls us back.

The Spider

When I appear to you
by dark, descended
not from heaven, but the lowest
branch of the walnut tree
bearing no annunciation,
suspended like a slub
in the air's weave
and you shriek, you shriek
so prettily, I'm reminded
of the birds – don't birds also
cultivate elaborate beauty, devour
what catches their eye?
Hence my night shift,
my sulphur-and-black-striped
jacket – *poison* – a lie
to cloak me while, exposed,
I squeeze from my own gut
the one material.
            Who tore the night?
Who caused this rupture?
You, staring in horror
 – had you never considered
how the world sustains?
The ants by day
clearing, clearing,
the spiders mending endlessly –

The Gather

The minute the men
ducked through the bothy door
they switched to English.
Even among themselves
they spoke English now,
out of courtesy,
and set about breakfast:
bread, bacon and sweet tea.
And are we enjoying
this weather, and whose
boat brought us, and what
part of the country – exactly –
would we be from ourselves?

– The tenant, ruddy-faced;
a strong bashful youngster,
and two old enough
to be their uncles,
who, planted at the wooden table
seemed happy for a bit crack:
– one with a horse-long,
marvellous weather
and nicotine-scored face
under a felt fedora,
whose every sentence
was a slow sea-wave
raking unhurriedly back

through the rounded
grey stones
at the landing place
where their boat was tied.

Beyond the bothy
– mended since the last gales –
the sea eased west
for miles toward the parishes,
hazy now,
the men had left early.
A sea settled for the meanwhile,
Aye, for the meanwhile!
Then, knocking their tea back,
they were out
round the gable end,
checking the sheep fanks, ready.

High on the island,
uninhabited these days, sheep
grazed oblivious,
till the dogs – the keenest
a sly, heavy-dugged bitch –
came slinking behind them.
Then men appeared, and that
backwash voice: *will you move
you baa-stards!*
Bleating in dismay
the animals zig-zagged down

the vertiginous hill
to spill onto the shore
where they ran, panicked,
and crammed into the fank:
heavy-fleeced mothers
and bewildered lambs,
from whom a truth,
(they now realized)
had been withheld.

'Ewe-lamb', 'tup-lamb',
each animal was seized,
its tail, severed with one snip,
shrugged through the air
to land in a red plastic pail;
each young tup,
upturned, took two men -
doubled over, heads together,
till the lamb's testicles
likewise thumped softly
into the tub, while we joked:
'Oh, will they no' mak a guid soup?'
No – we will deep-fry them,
like they do in Glaa-sgow
with the Maa-rs bars!
Then thrust, one by one
to the next pen, the lambs
huddled in a corner,
and with blood dribbling
down their sturdy

little thighs, they jumped
very lightly, as though in joy.

Summer was passing:
just above the waves,
guillemots whirred toward
their cliff-ledge nests,
but they carried nothing;
few young, this year –
Aye, the birds –
not so many now . . .
and the men stood, considering.
Then it was the ewes:
each in turn, a man's thumb
crossways in her mouth
was tilted upside down
like a small sofa, and clipped
till she stepped out trig
and her fleece
cast over the side:
Fit only to be burned! –
No market nowadays –

All the hot Saturday
the men kept to their work
– a modest living –
pausing every so often
to roll cigarettes, or tilt
plastic bottles of cola
to their parched mouths,

as their denims and tee-shirts
turned slowly rigid
with sweat and wool-grease
and the tide began to lift
fronds of dark weed
as though seeking
something mislaid,
and from the cliffs,
through the constant bleating
came the wild birds'
faint, strangulated cries.

When, late in the day
they were done, the sheep,
began to pick their way
up to their familiar pastures –
first the old ewes,
who understood
– if anything – that they,
who take but a small share,
are a living, whom
now and then
a fate visits, like a storm.

But though the sky
was still blue with
teased out clouds,
and the sea brimmed and
lapped at the shore rocks gently,
and they could have rested,

the men wanted away
before the wind rose,
before – they laughed –
the taverns close!
And I run out of tob-aacco!
Before – though they didn't
actually say this – the Sabbath,
so they loaded their boat
– a RIB with a hefty outboard –
and hauled the dogs in.
At first they chugged out
slow and old-fashioned,
like a scene in a documentary,

but suddenly with an arched,
overblown plume
of salt spray
they roared off at top speed,
throwing us a grand wave.

Roses

for M D

This is the moment the roses
cascade over backstreet walls,
throng the public parks –
their cream or scrunched pinks

unfolding now to demonstrate
unacknowledged thought.
The world is ours too! they brave,
careless of tomorrow

and wholly without leadership
for who'd mount a soap-box
on the rose-behalf?

'I haggle for my little
portion of happiness,'
says each flower, equal, in the scented mass.

The Overhaul

Look – it's the *Lively*,
hauled out above the tideline
up on a trailer with two
flat tyres. What –

14 foot? Clinker-built
and chained by the stern
to a pile of granite blocks,
but with the bow

still pointed westward
down the long voe,
down toward the ocean,
where the business is.

Inland from the shore
a road runs, for the crofts
scattered on the hill
where washing flaps,

and the school bus calls
and once a week or so
the mobile library;
but see how this

duck-egg green keel's
all salt-weathered,
how the stem, taller
– like a film star –

than you'd imagine,
is raked to hold steady
if a swell picks up
and everyone gets scared . . .

No, it can't be easy,
when the only spray to touch
your boards all summer
is flowers of scentless mayweed;

when little wavelets leap
less than a stone's throw
with your good name
written all over them –

but hey, *Lively*,
it's a time-of-life thing,
it's a waiting game –
patience, patience.

Halfling

Bird on the cliff-top,
the angle of your back
a master-stroke:
why should kittiwakes

plunge at your head
with white shrills?
You're only just falling
from your parents' care,

they've dared slope off
together, to quarter
the island's only glen
leaving you sunlit, burnished,

glaring out to sea
like one bewildered.
Some day soon you'll
topple to the winds

and be gone, a gangrel,
obliged to wander
island to mountain,
taking your chances —

till you moult at last
to an adult's mantle
and settle some scant
estate of your own. Already

the gulls shriek *Eagle!*
Eagle!—they know
more than you
what you'll become.

An Avowal

Bluebell at the wayside
nodding your assent
to summer, and summer's end;
nodding, on your slender stem

your undemurring *yes*
to the small role life
offers you – a few weeks
seasoning the hill-foot grasses

with shakes of blue . . .
You accept, and acquiesce
thereby, to any wind,
though the winds tease:

'Flower,' they ask –
'd'you want to be noticed?'
Yes, yes, noticed!
'Or rather left alone?' *Yes,*

left perfectly alone! 'Flower,'
they whisper, 'd'you love
the breeze that wantons
the whole earth round

breathing its sweet proposals,
but does not love you?'
 — then laugh when your blue
head nods: *I do. I do.*

The Galilean Moons

for Nat Jansz

Low in the south sky shines
the stern white lamp
of planet Jupiter. A man
on the radio said
it's uncommonly close;
sequestered in the telescope lens
it's like a compere, spotlit,
driving its borrowed light
out to all sides equally.
While set in a row in the dark
beyond its blaze,
like seed-pearls,
or coy new talents
awaiting their call onstage –
are what must be, surely,
the Galilean moons.

In another room,
my children lie asleep, turning
as Earth turns, growing
into their own lives, leaving me
a short time to watch, eye
to the eye-piece,
how a truth unfolds –
how the moonlets glide

out of their chance alignment,
each again to describe
around its shared host
its own unalterable course.

Tell me, Galileo, is this
what we're working for?
The knowing that in just
one Jovian year
the children will be gone
uncommonly far, their bodies
aglow, grown, talented –
mere bright voice-motes
calling from the opposite
side of the world.
What else would we want
our long-sighted instruments
to assure us of? I'd like
to watch for hours, see
what you old astronomers
apprehended for the first time,
bowing to the inevitable . . .

but it's late. Already
the next day
plucks at my elbow
like a wakeful infant,
next-door's dog barks,
and a cloud arrives,
appearing out of nothing.

The Bridge

Mind thon bridge? The wynds
that spawned us? Those hemmed in,
ramshackle tenements
taller, it seemed, every year . . .

Caller herrin'! Ony rags! On the mountain
stands a lady . . .
What a racket! Coal smoke,
midden-reek . . . filthy,

needless to mention, our two
old hives, heaped high
either side of the river,
crammed with the living, with the dead-beat

and joined by that sandstone ligature . . .
Did you ever notice
how walking out over the water
made us more human:

men became gracious,
women unfolded
their arms from their breasts –
and where else could children,

beggars, any one of us,
pause and look up at the sky!
And that river! Forever
bearing its breeze to the sea,

like a rustic bride, scented
now with blossom,
now with pine sap,
— But what was the sea to us, then?

What was a mountain?
Yes; us. Me and you. *That* bridge,
long ago demolished
where we first met.

Tae the Fates

eftir Hölderlin

Gie me, ye Po'ers, jist ane simmer mair
an ane maumie autumn,
that ma hairt, ripe wi sweet sang,
's no sae swier for tae dee. A sowl

denied in life its heevinly richt
wil waunner Orcus disjaiskit;
but gin ah could mak whit's halie
an maist dear tae me – ane perfect poem

I'll welcome the cauld, the quate mirk!
For though I maun lee' ma lyre
an gang doon wantin sang, Ah'd hae lived,
aince, lik the gods; and aince is eneuch.

Moon

Last night, when the moon
slipped into my attic-room
as an oblong of light,
I sensed she'd come to commiserate.

It was August. She travelled
with a small valise
of darkness, and the first few stars
returning to the northern sky,

and my room, it seemed,
had missed her. She pretended
an interest in the bookcase
while other objects

stirred, as in a rockpool,
with unexpected life:
strings of beads in their green bowl gleamed,
the paper-crowded desk;

the books, too, appeared inclined
to open and confess.
Being sure the moon
harboured some intention,

I waited; watched for an age
her cool gaze shift
first toward a flower sketch
pinned on the far wall

then glide to recline
along the pinewood floor
before I'd had enough. *Moon,*
I said, *we're both scarred now.*

Are they quite beyond you,
the simple words of love? Say them.
You are not my mother;
with my mother, I waited unto death.

The Lighthouse

Here is the lighthouse,
redundant these days.
From the keepers'
neglected garden
– the sea, of course
a metallic seam
closing the horizon.
– And gulls too,
uttering the same
torn-throated cries
as when you first imagined
hours spent hunched
against the wind-
abraded wall might yield some
species of understanding.
All those hours, gazing
out to the ocean.
Years ago now.

Glamourie

When I found I'd lost you –
not beside me, nor ahead,
nor right nor left not
your green jacket moving

between the trees anywhere –
I waited a long while
before wandering on. No wren
jinked in the undergrowth,

not a twig snapped.
It was hardly the Wildwood –
just some auld fairmer's
shelter belt – but red haws

reached out to me,
and between fallen leaves
pretty white flowers bloomed
late into their year. I tried

calling out, or think
I did, but your name
shrivelled on my tongue,
so instead I strolled on

through the wood's good
offices, and duly fell
to wondering if I hadn't
simply made it all up. You,

I mean, everything,
my entire life. Either way,
nothing now could touch me
bar my hosts, who appeared

as diffuse golden light,
as tiny spiders
examining my hair . . .
What gratitude I felt then –

I might be gone for ages,
maybe seven years! –
and such sudden joie de vivre
that when a ditch gaped

right there instantly in front of me
I jumped it, blithe as a girl –
ach, I jumped clear over it,
without even pausing to think.

The Roost

Dusk, and the black rooks
rise from their stubble-fields,
returning to the pine-copse
they quit at dawn.

Kaah . . . kaah . . . kaah . . . they proclaim
their shared release,
straggling in loose groups
above hedges and the river

as though the trees
were singing, to draw them in.
They go; the peasant earth
they've probed all day

beneath them now,
and of no matter.
There are only the trees
luring from their realms of sky

each mite of darkness
to counter the coming night;
and *kaah . . . kaah . . . kaah . . .*
the rooks reply.

The Wood

She comes to me
as a jay's shriek,
as ragged branches shading
deerways I find myself

lost among for days,
weeks, till the crisis
passes. When I weep
she strokes my hair

and calls me 'babe',
coaxing me to fall
once more for her
scarlet-berry promises –

This time, she says, *I'll keep you,*
so you'll never have to face them all again.

The Whales

If I could stand the pressures,
if I could make myself strong,

I'd dive far under the ocean,
away from these merfolk

– especially the mermen, moaning
and wringing out their beards.

I'd discover a cave
green and ventricular

and there, with tremendous patience,
I'd teach myself to listen:

what the whale-fish hear
answering through the vastnesses

I'd hear too. But oh my love,
tell me you'd swim by,

tell me you'd look out for me,
down there it's impossible to breathe –

The Widden Burd

i.m. ITJ

Nae lang yirdit
but here y'ur back —
turnt tae a blackie
feathert in bark —

Nou ye ken whit befaa's
folk that wad clype
on whit tends tae us aa
ayont the dyke —

a burnt gleg ee,
twa wire feet,
a thrapple o wid
that cannae wheep

fi the heighest branch
o' ony tree . . . Och
how could ye no'
hae gane quaitely?

Hauf o' Life

eftir Hölderlin

Bien wi yella pears, fu
o wild roses, the braes
fa intil the loch;
ye mensefu' swans,
drunk wi kisses
dook yir heids
i' the douce, the hailie watter.

But whaur when winter's wi us
will ah fin flo'ers?
Whaur the shadda
an sunlicht o the yird?
Dumbfounert, the wa's staun.
The cauld blast
claitters the wethervanes.

Even the Raven

The grey storm passes
a storm the sea wakes from
then soon forgets . . .

surf plumes at the rocks –
wave after wave, each
drawing its own long fetch

– and the hills across the firth –
golden, as the cloud lifts – yes
it's here, everything

you wanted, everything
you insisted on –

Even the raven,
his old crocked voice

asks you what you're waiting for

Materials

for C.M.

See when it all unravels – the entire project
reduced to threads of moss fleeing a nor'wester;
d'you ever imagine chasing just one strand, letting it lead you
to an unsung cleft in a rock, a place you could take to,
dig yourself in – but what are the chances of that?
                                                    Of the birds,
few remain all winter; half a dozen waders
mediate between sea and shore, that space confirmed
– don't laugh – by your own work. Waves boom, off-white
spume-souls twirl out of geos, and look,

blown about the headland: scraps of nylon fishing net. Gannets
– did you know? – pluck such rubbish from the waves, then
          hie awa'
to colonies so raucous and thief-ridden, each nest
winds up swagged to the next . . . Then they're flown, and the
          cliff's left
wearing naught but a shoddy, bird-knitted vest.

And look at us! Out all day and damn all to show for it.
Bird-bones, rope-scraps, a cursory sketch – but a bit o' bruck's
all we need to get us started, all we'll leave behind us when
          we're gone.

ACKNOWLEDGEMENTS

I am grateful to the editors of the following journals,
in which some of these poems first appeared.

Edinburgh Review, the *Guardian*, *Irish Pages*,
the *London Review of Books*, *Orion*, the *New Yorker*,
Poetry London, *Poetry Review*, *Woodlanders*.
'The Beach' was broadcast on BBC Radio 3.

The quotation in 'Roses' is from Rosa Luxemburg.

With special thanks to James Dodds for his lino-cut,
'Shetland Fourern'.

ACKNOWLEDGEMENTS

I am grateful to the editors of the following journals, in which some of these poems first appeared.

Edinburgh Review, the *Guardian*, *Irish Pages*, the *London Review of Books*, *Orion*, the *New Yorker*, *Poetry London*, *Poetry Review*, *Woodlanders*. 'The Beach' was broadcast on BBC Radio 3.

The quotation in 'Roses' is from Rosa Luxemburg.

With special thanks to James Dodds for his lino-cut, 'Shetland Fourern'.

KATHLEEN JAMIE was born in the west of
Scotland in 1962. She is the author of six previous
poetry collections, including *Waterlight: Selected
Poems*. *The Overhaul* won the Costa Prize and
was shortlisted for the T. S. Eliot Prize. Jamie's
nonfiction books include the highly regarded
Findings and *Sightlines,* which won the John
Burroughs Medal and the Orion Book Award.
She is chair of creative writing at Stirling
University, and lives with her family in Fife,
Scotland.

The Overhaul is set in Apollo MT.
Manufactured by Versa Press on acid-free,
30 percent postconsumer wastepaper.